AF454251

CAST IN A WICKED STONE

Helle Gade

BUTTERDRAGONS
PUBLISHING

Title: Cast in a Wicked Stone

Author: Helle Gade

Copyright © 2024 Butterdragons® Publishing

All Rights Reserved

Published by Butterdragons® Publishing
https://butterdragons.com

ISBN: 9789493287365 (ebook)
ISBN: 9789493287372 (hardback)
ISBN: 9789493287389 (audio book)

Cover Design by: Dazed Designs

Audio book narrated by Martha Webb

For Helle, with love

The world is grey and darkness all around. The colours faded with time. Heart heavy and depressed with each passing moment.

You see words of other which are hard and full of criticism. You wish to break free for all that surround you.

A candle in the darkness appears. Others gather to her like a moth to a flame. She enfolds the masses with her loving works and tender heart.

She is an artist not of paint or photography, but of words so powerful, that the colours and the feeling bloom within.

She is a loving master, one who guides and encourages, all who inspire to fly among her ranks. To paint the world with words that inspire vivid colour and hope for all.

by BDP Authors

Tired

I play hide and seek with my demons

I think they are cheating

I keep losing

Chatter

I wish I could retreat
Into the catacombs of my mind
Where peace and quiet rule

Instead, I must suffer
Through the incessant chatter of my brain
Nagging me constantly

On and on, it goes
Sleep, a distant wish
Rest, a hopeless dream

Sleep Paralysis

My sleep is haunted

By the paralysis demon

He covers me like a blanket

Preventing me from moving

He hugs me like a lover

Refusing to let me go

Panic is suffocating me

Making it hard to breathe

I silently yell and rage against him

Trying to move my body

But I can't, no matter how hard I try

Not even a twitch of my fingers

And when he finally releases me

I feel like I have run a marathon

No rest for my tortured body

Tired, I crawl out of my bed

Afraid to sleep again

Afraid of being haunted again

Spoonies

My cries are unheard
My pain unknown
My struggles unseen
I stand in a sea of people
Silently raging for not being seen
Yet, I would rather hide
Instead of explaining myself
Again

I know I am not alone
Many walk the same path
Preserving their precious energy
To fight each day
United under the banner
Of chronic illness
Alone

Caught In Terror

Something is stalking me in the night
Exuding sinister vibes
That slither over my skin

Terror crawls through my body
Like a living entity
With claws and venom

It has me tossing and turning
My bed, now, a prison
Preventing me from waking

Yellow Light

Breathing rapidly, covered in cold sweat
Tangled in the covers of my bed
My mind silenced by the pulsating pain

Flowing like violent waves
Lapping at my skin like fire
Stabbing like a dagger or an ice pick
Or a million needles piercing me at once

Shifting between hot and cold sweats
Skin sensitive like after a sunburn
Restless legs dancing
Nerves dipped in acid

Thankfully it doesn't happen
All at the same time
Or madness would have
Claimed me by now

Yet my body never lets me forget
It's never numb or pain free
It is snapping at the air like a scared dog
Running constantly at yellow light

Woman!

I am a Woman!
You might have taken my power
When I was young
And still possessed innocence
But now, I have reclaimed it

I still have insecurities
But I'm sure
I can eradicate all
That crept into my mind
When I was otherwise occupied

I am a Woman!
I'm stronger because
I don't give a damn anymore
Pain, fatigue, and mental issues
Have stripped me of energy to care
What others think of me

I have learned to care for me

For the comfort of my body and mind

I have grown beyond the worries

Of what the others think is best

My home is my safe space

I am a Woman!

I own my power now

And no one can take it away

Succeeding Jealously

It is hard to see other people
With disabilities and chronic illnesses
Succeed out there, among people
Working on their happiness
And managing their health

It makes me feel inadequate
It makes me fear that others
Will expect more from me
More than I am able to give

I do not begrudge their success
I applaud it and wish I could do the same
They give me hope I might some day
Yet, I have to fight my jealousy at times
Because I'm scared I might not

A Little Peace

Sometimes
I just Want to hold my breath
Until the pain leaves me be
Yet, it rarely works

My body is stuck
In a perpetual circle of alarm
Reacting to the smallest changes
Punishing me for the smallest infractions

I just want to exist
Without having to
Constantly fight for air
In peace with myself

Tired

I am tired as f*ck

Of scheduling everything

Of writing lists

Of trying to remember things

So, I can manage

To complete my chores

I can't even remember

What it's like to be spontaneous

To rush out the door to meet friends

Or just to go for a walk

All needs to be scheduled now

So, I can be back before my body gives out

And when the time comes again

For me to go out

I just want to hide under the covers

Being stressed is now a norm

Even before I go out the door

My memory is shot

My body is broken

Nothing is simple anymore

Spontaneity is a thing of the past

Numb

The side effects are strong tonight
Life is blurry around the edges
As if my senses were covered in cotton

At least the pain is temporarily gone
But I know it is only a short reprieve
Before it hits me again

The painkillers don't always help
They don't work on my treacherous body
I'm sentenced to perpetual agony

Iris

It came out of the blue
Yet another illness
Nothing terminal but still scary
With possible repercussions
The pain it had caused me
Brought me to my knees
It left me fragile and hurting
In the darkness of my nest

Sun and light
Felt like sharp knives
Causing panic and stress
To ravage my body
Until finally, a blessed relief came
Brought by the grace of angels in white coats

Hollow

Sometimes I wish
That I could sleep
Through the daylight
Until night falls
And true darkness reigns

It cocoons me so softly
Like a warm blanket
Over my frayed senses
Allowing me true rest
A restoration of body and soul

Yet, when morning light returns
I feel the fatigue
Deep in my bones
As I wrestle with the simplest of tasks
Feeling exhausted and hollow

Draining

I'm tired, so tired
Sometimes, I just sit here
Staring at nothing
Contemplating things
I can't accomplish

I wish I could just
Shut off my mind for a moment
Stop my thoughts from churning
Like a never-ending storm
Draining my precious energy

Yet I still sit there
Fidgeting
Never still
Never calm
Never restful

Insanity

Malady

It's killing me slowly, this malady
I feel it burning in my veins
I feel it festering under my skin

My mind corrodes with my body
Terrible thoughts consume me
Begging me to act them out

But I just lie here in my bed
Letting the delirium ravage me
As the sickness devours
my soon to be corpse

Bloody Dreams

I dream of blood

Death and dismemberment

Of the silent soul

Falling over the edge

In the dark hours

Of the winter nights

I dream of him

Of flesh falling off his bones

Decay of his humanity

As insanity takes over

Bleeding him dry

Of all that he is

I dream of the pleasure

This gives me

As death caresses my cheek

His approval imperative

While we both wait

For the inevitable to come

Voices

Acid runs down my throat
Corroding everything on its way

They told me to do it, the voices, you know
The ones that I have carried with me, always

Mooooore, they gleefully yell in my head
And I give them more, pouring it all over

They didn't tell me it would smell this way
This disgusting odour

Receiving a standing ovation from them
As I am dissolving upon the concrete

I wonder if they will follow me into death
Or find a new victim to corrupt?

Restrained

Prodding, probing
I feel along the jagged edge
Of the festering wound
In my ailing soul

The declining sanity
Brings beguiling urges of death
And rivers of blood
Caused by my hands

If only I could move
Frome these restraints
Locking me to a gurney
In an endlessly white room

Alpträume

I lie in the dark
Listening to the whispers
That flow over the city
As sleep claims its victims

What started out as
Hopes and dreams
Twists into dark illusions
That taunt the humans

There is no rest for the wicked
In this frightful night
There is no rest for the pietist
As hope dies a slow death

All that is left

A writhing pit of souls

Feeding the greedy

Feeding the corrupt

Black Blood

The blood runs down the walls
Of my prison cell
Madness leaking out of my pores
The pain unbearable
Yet, I crave it passionately

I carve it into my flesh
I carve it into my soul

I rake my nails over the walls
Screaming... howling...

I see you watch me with malice
Enjoying my painful malady
Wishing you were the one to break me
But no, I will not let you have that pleasure

This is my insanity, my abyss
My delightful death approaching

Us

You bring out the stars in my eyes
And the love in my heart

You bring out the best in me
And the worst

You love me and hate me
As I do you

Our wills clash with
Thunder and ice

Bringing down worlds
With our passion

Razing the lands with our wrath
Ripping hope from the heart

I will love you forever

I will hate you equally so

Wild Hunt

It crawls towards me
Under the cover of nightfall
Leaving a trail of death in its wake

As it reaches my feet
Writhing in happiness
Whining in anticipation
I gently stroke its furry head
I understand its eager shaking
The hunt begins when bell tolls

We will bathe in blood this night
Dancing in the remains of the wicked
Celebrating the evil we have vanquished

Bloodletting

I carve a pattern of distasteful images
On one of my thighs

I watch in fascination as the skin splits open
Eying my flesh to see the corruption

A trail of vermillion falling to the floor
Making an obscene sound

Bliss....bliss....bliss.....

My demons are frolicking in my mind
In this, we are in complete agreement

One more cut, or maybe two?
To prolong the dreamy silence

Surrender

His touch is a persistent craving
That I cannot let myself indulge in

His smoky voice dark and rich
Lulling my mind into bliss

Right before he rips out my heart
Tearing it into shreds with gleaming claws

I have no defences
Against his seductive allure

It pulls me in as surely
As the tide follows the moon

No begging or pleading
Will save me from heartbreak

He will destroy me violently
And leave me in broken pieces

So, I surrender my body and soul
To his cruel brand of love

Dance With Me

We dance in the blood
And revel in insanity

Claws and talons
Fangs and flesh

You draw me
Into your delusions

Pulling me apart
Until only bones are left

A quivering mass
Of unstable emotions

Clinging to those bones
Without apology

Deranged

I see your scars
Angry red lines
Covering you
Matching mine
Like a mirror image
Or mutual madness
Our souls jagged
Yet fitting like a bizarre puzzle
Courting deranged delights
As the darkness claims us

Chaos

We breathe the polluted hatred
Poisoning our world
With filthy lies and deceit

We swim in the waste of the rich soil
Ripping off our humanity
Showing the dark promises of agony

We fight for our right to bring chaos
Dancing in the blood of our enemies
As we die a little bit by little bit inside

Witch

The sweet breath of poison
I swallow down with relish

Datura and mandrake
Making me fly high

On broom and in spirit
I traverse realms with joy

A touch of madness
And old gods gathering

Deal

I made a deal with the Devil
Signing away my soul

It was a cheap price to pay
After what was done to me
At the hands of love

Now I swing the scythe
With relish and precision

Maidens of Madness

Salem

Madness, murder, and moral decay
Is what I crave with a silent appetite
Rolling in it like a witch's cat
High on catnip at midnight

I wish to dance in the warm blood
To celebrate the ending
Of the corrosion of society's standards
Like a maiden of Salem
Burned at the stake

Weak Egos

I feel the skin split to the bone
As the whip lashes at my back

Blood and grime running down
Over my buttocks, down my thighs

After this amount of lashes
I no longer feel a thing

Darkness encroaches on my vision
Promising peace at least

I wonder when we, women, lost
The divine power over our soul and bodies

Another lash landing on my lower back
Ripping the skin with a dreadful sound

It is getting darker, harder to breathe
Harder to collect my precious thoughts

We were once free, with a beautiful legacy
Left by countless women fighting

Now, we are once again enslaved
Under the whims of insecure men

Like the one stripping the flesh from my back
Because he couldn't handle the word NO

Society

I sit here watching my heart palpitate
Through the massive hole in my chest

Hands clutching my ribcage
Pulling, ripping, digging

The pain screaming through my system
Making my heart beat faster

My voice long gone
My will to live abandoned me

Yet, I still live in this nightmarish moment
Tortured by the wet and cracking sounds

I vaguely see him hovering nearby
The Reaper who awaits my death

I would love to oblige him

But that is a silly wish

These horrid blood-coated fiends

Are not yet done with me and my agony

My scream is silent

My pain immeasurable

Hunter

Branches and brambles
Scratching my skin
Pulling at my clothes
As I run breathlessly
Through the forest

I can feel the hunter
Not far behind
Getting closer
As I slowly lose ground
Terror running through my veins

If he catches me
He will kill me
Slowly and with excruciating pain
There will be no mercy

Boogeywoman

I was once innocent

I was once alive

Now, I'm dead inside

My heart shrivelled and black

I haunt the streets in the shadows

Feared by the entities living there

The Boogywoman they call me

And that is what I have become

I Am

I am the sun
Playful and social

I am the winter nights
Covered in a cosy blanket
With books and tea

I am the witching hour
Where my demons dance

I am the crisp hoarfrost morning
Bundled up in coat and scarf
With a camera in hand

I am the grey rainy day
Lost in the search of happiness

I am the hour of the wolf
The time for new souls
And old souls to part

I am the primordial element
Consisting of sparkling stardust

Dangerous Path

A chameleon is what he is
He carries an androgynous beauty
That can turn masculine within a single beat

He flows between innocence
And sensuality
With calculated moves

You think you know him
But that is far from the truth
Shrouded in shadows as he is

He lures you in with glimpses
Of beauty and strength
Snaring you in his web

He entices you

Out of your comfort zone

Into dangerous waters

Entices you to let it all go

To trust in him

Even though your instincts flare

Beauty Idols

We fight for them to notice us

With layers of makeup and shape wear

Trying to hide our flaws

That make us uniquely us

Carrying our insecurities

Into domed relationships

When do we say enough is enough?

When do we stop emulating

Rich social media celebrities

That airbrush and photoshop everything

Teaching young girls

That being themselves is wrong

They starve themselves

Spend all their money on makeup

Anxious because they can't be "perfect"

Depressed due to feeling like failures

Portray their lives online as ideal
As they fall apart behind the screen
Because they don't have "enough" followers

When do we take care of the girls cutting
themselves?
The ones that become suicidal because they
can't achieve what their idols have
Or the ones that get bullied for not following
the trends of social media

I am disgusted by the creators
Disinterested in the influence
They have on their followers

Hear Me Roar

They say that this is
A patriarchal society

They say we are
The weaker sex

They try to take away
Our choices
To rule our bodies
To live our lives

But Hell No, I say

We are fierce
We are fabulous
We are the power
That makes the world turn

Through us, future generations
Will emerge victorious

Through us, they will learn
Love, compassion, and equality

Hurricane

I am standing in the eye of the hurricane
Not a breeze to tease my hair
Not a sound to caress my ear

Everything is momentarily frozen
In a violent silence
Promising further devastation

All is deadly still before the hurricane
Yet again erupt with a brutal force
Of Mother Earth's wrath and sorrow

I feel the abuse of her sacred lands
The tears she weeps for her children
Even though cause her pain

I Wonder

I watch your lips as you speak
Wondering how soft they are

Maybe as soft as your words
Or teasing like the glint in your eyes

Or maybe as hard as your actions
When you conquer your adversaries

I wonder if you will scream
Like the women you have hurt

I wonder if you will feel the pain and fright
Your victims were imbued with

When I seek revenge for the lost souls
Failed by the system

Gentle Salvation

She's a goddess in the making
Rising from the earth as a cool star

She moves to the sound
Of the wolves howling at full moon

She is something new
In this godless world

She brings hope where there is none
Embracing mankind with love

She embraces humanity
As humans destroy their future

She carries her children in her heart
Towards the final destination

Hateful Love

Pretty Smiles

Dark are the powers
That show the prettiest smiles

They hide the ugly truth
Of their malignant souls

They seduce you with sweet words
While plotting behind your back

You fall into their beauty
Surrendering yourself to their deception

Leaving you open for heartbreak
And lasting consequences

Some will learn and rise above them
Others will be trapped in that vicious circle

Love Hurts

I would die for you...
What a declaration of love
You might think

No, I want you alive
To see the pain in your eyes
As love breaks your spirit

When you feel like
Your heart is exposed
For the world to see

The raging madness
Beats within this bloody
Cardiovascular organ

Our love is haunting
I see the sky burning
In your pain filled eyes

Yet, you annihilated
My hopeful heart
Before we even had begun

So, I tied myself to you
Until you only had love
For me in your heart

And now, I watch with joy
As Karma peals you apart
Layer by distasteful layer

The revenge is tasting sweet
With a hint of rot
Yet, I enjoy it fully

Twenty

One two

I saw you

Three four

I loved before

Five six

You were my eclipse

Seven eight

I carried your weight

Nine ten

Though before then

Eleven twelve

I was compelled

Thirteen fourteen

You were my morphine

Fifteen sixteen

I tried to get clean

Seventeen eighteen

I thought I was your queen

Nineteen twenty

But you hurt me plenty

Burn

You burned my bridges
You ripped me apart
You unmade what I have accomplished
With vicious words and malice

But you did not expect me
To rise from the ashes
With vengeance in my hart
And murder in my soul

I want to break you
I want to tear down your walls
And pick you apart piece by piece
Until there is only your black heart left

I will save your heart

In a black box on my mantle

Reminding me to never ever

Let myself be fooled again

Filthy Lies

As I drink the bitter truth
Of the poison it promised
I see you for the devil you are

A careless bastard
Selfish and cruel
Only focusing on you

Your honeyed words
Were nothing but filthy lies
Tarnishing me with deceit

And I fell for it
I gobbled it all up
Like a starving creature

Letting it fill my soul

With empty promises

And toxic hope

I imagine that

You lie to yourself as well

To be able to sleep at night

I hope, that one day

You'll feel the sting of Karma

As she gives you back threefold

Frost

Silver slivers of pain

Radiating frozen through my bones

Glacier melting down my spine

A snowstorm that threatens

To rip the flesh of my bones

Frost coating my lunges

Threatening to choke me

I thought he was my salvation

My saving grace

In this desolate wasteland of cold

Sensual Shadows

A Devil

His kiss is slow and soft
Drawing forth a soft moan

He is enchanting in his seduction
Alluring and daunting in its intensity

I'm a breath away
From sweet death

In the arms of the devil
I surrender myself to his love

Chained Sensuality

They look at each other
With suspicious curiosity

Their looks blending
Demanding answers

Attraction burning
Through their veins

A scalding wave of red
Stoking the fire higher

Yet none of them gives in
Their strengths keeping them apart

Frustration unleashed

In a flurry of violent movements

As they draw nearer to each other

Pulling each other's strings

Delights of the Devil

He trails his finger up my arm
Goosebumps following its path

A slow smile spreading on his face
At the power of his touch

I try to deny his seductive allure
Knowing it will bring pain

He draws me to his chest
Refusing to let me go

Dragging me deeper
Into his soulless eyes

Unleashing the madness
I carry within my soul

We waltz on the coals of hell
Tiny flames licking our dark hearts

Unleashing a passion
That could destroy worlds

Pleasures of the demons within
Sensual delights on the sacrificial altar

We share fiery breaths
As the gods accept our token

The agony envelops us in its embrace
Tearing our insides into bloody ribbons

Killing us slowly
Hurting so good

Euphoria

I have loved and lost
I have fought battles
Against dragons and demons
I have danced in the rain
Singing songs of freedom

I have weathered storms at sea
Battering my senses to pieces
Coming out stronger afterwards
But I never saw you coming

You swept me of my feet
With your seductive kisses
Your sensual and daring touches
Whispers promising euphoria

I writhe beneath your attention

Letting you play me

Like a finely tuned instrument

Creating a crescendo of ecstasy

Fire and Water

You watch me sleep

Moonbeams caressing my naked flesh

Tracing every curve with your eyes

Memorising the landscape of my body

For the times we are apart

And the times we fight

We are fire and water

An unlikely pair

Meeting in a frenzy of burning skin

And teeth clashing

Cutting our lips

Yet not stopping us

I feel the claw marks you left on my back
I will relish the memory
Of how I got them
When I leave you in the morning

If Only

I watch you under my lashes
Imagining your hands on my skin
Your breath in my ear
As you whisper every single thing
You intend to torment me with

Hands above my head
Your hand holding them tight
Your thigh pressed between my legs
Pinning me firmly to the wall
Towering over my slight frame

If only I had the courage
To approach you
To see if you have the darkness
I crave so passionately
But I stay in the shadows, watching

Mania

Dazed desires
Running rampant
As he moves
To the beat of my heart
Tugging my heartstrings

Sweet venom flows in his veins
Bleeding into my skin
As our bodies undulate
In an ancient mating ritual
Ment for goddesses and gods

Yet, we defile the old ways
With new toxins
Creating new gods
To worship mania
And bloody battles

Mine

His pale eyes
See right through me
Stripping my soul bare
For him to devour

I offer it to him freely
Pain be damned
Because the agony
He carries within
Will be mine to shatter

Butterflies

They move together
As if they are one being

Their bodies sinuous
Undulating to the music

Staring into each other's eyes
Completely focused on the moment

They pull you into their bubble
Making you envious of their closeness

Making your breathing hitch
And you stomach fill with butterflies

Seduction

She is fire encased in sin
Voluptuous and violent

She is seduction incarnate
Sensual and addictive

She is the slow drip of blood
From a deep wound

She is the poison
You crave with your heart and soul

She destroys you bit by bit
With every touch, every kiss

She is the one you will bleed for
The one you will die for

Time

Breaths mingled

Skin against skin

Limbs entangled

In an everlasting dance

As old as time itself

Tropical Nights

The tropical sultry night air

Replaces the humid

Feel of the day

Awakening the soul

Now it's time to move

To dance the night away

Writhing bodies move

With joyful abandon

The music brings them into

A transcendental state of mind

All worries forgotten

They live in the Here and Now

Waves

You push and pull me
Through waves of emotions

The water caressing my soul
Cooling and heating

Love and hate blend
Until I cannot tell them apart

Yet, I crave more
I demand more

Give me everything you have
Let me float in the sea of bliss
You create with your rough demands
And callus hands

Primal

His body moving like air

Light as a feather

He dances like the elements

A beautiful storm of movement

His body flowing like water

Over all shapes of rocks

One moment hard and striking

Next soft and smooth

The kinetic energy streaming

In a push-and-pull motion

Of the moon and madness

The sensuality he exudes

Translates directly

Into gasping breaths of lunacy

Up and down as the dancer

Tells his story with his whole body

I can feel what he is trying to convey

Interpreting it my way as I watch

Satisfying a primal part of me

That now understands it is not alone

Leaving me in a languid state of mind

Beautiful Death

Oh, beautiful Death

Can you not hear my silent cries?

Can you not see my tears?

Can you not feel my yearning

To walk by your side in the shadows

Forever shrouded in darkness

Oh, beautiful Death

I beg you to listen

To feel me, to see me

To embrace my tortured soul

As we dance along the road of bones

Forever entwined in the fire of the Universe

Hot and Cold

She belongs amongst the stars

Her light too bright

For mortal eyes

Unique like a snowflake

He's a smouldering volcano

A fiery soul on the inside

A calm unmoving

Mountain on the outside

Their joining is cataclysmic

Fire and ice clashing

In a ground shaking explosion

My Moon

A blushing Moon
Travelling beyond
A deep yearning
Coming from within

You touched my soul
And owned my heart
For a split second
In a vast Universe

A hunger like no other
A stolen moment

Hear me above the stars
Feel me in the shadows
Drink me in under the nebula
Hold on to me forever

Acknowledgements

Thank you, Ira, for always keeping me present and making me laugh hard enough to accidentally fart.

Raymond, thank you for sharing your inner Wookie.

Thank you, my fellow spoonies, for your constant support. You are all warriors!

About Helle Gade

Helle Gade is a modern-day Danish Viking. She suffers from a chronic illness and all the delights that come with it, so she self-medicates with liberal amounts of chocolate.

When she started writing poetry in 2011, she found a perfect outlet for all her bottled-up emotions, and since apparently there were plenty, she has published numerous poetry collection since then, with more coming. Her book Nocturnal Embers won the Best Poetry Collection with eFestival of Words.

She loves staying up all night immersing herself in the wonderful worlds of books. When she's not buried in a book, she is busy with photography and book blogging.

Other BDP books by Helle Gade

How To Tame A Wild Tempest

The Fighter

Dolce Amore

Spirit

Urban Rose

Collection of Poems from Books

Collection of Scary Love Stories

Collection of Tragic Love Stories

Collection of Suspenseful Tattoo Stories